CONSTELLATIONS

A TRUE BOOK

by
**Diane M. Sipiera and
Paul P. Sipiera**

Children's Press®
A Division of Grolier Publishing

New York London Hong Kong Sydney
Danbury, Connecticut

Stars of the Big
Dipper above Mono
Lake in California

Reading Consultant
Linda Cornwell
Learning Resource Consultant
Indiana Department of
Education

Science Consultant
Samuel Storch
Lecturer,
American Museum-Hayden
Planetarium, New York City

Dedicated to the memory
of Mary Vidmar,
Diane's grandmother,
her inspiration

Library of Congress Cataloging-in-Publication Data

Sipiera, Diane M.
    Constellations / by Diane M. Sipiera and Paul P. Sipiera
        p.   cm. — (A true book)
    Includes bibliographical references and index.
    Summary: Identifies the groups of stars known as constellations and
discusses their origin, uses, and observation.
    ISBN 0-516-20331-2 (lib.bdg.)   0-516-26167-3 (pbk.)
    1. Constellations — Juvenile literature. [1. Constellations.] I. Sipiera,
Paul P. II. Title. III. Series.
QB801.7.S57 1997
523.8'022'3—dc20   96-28555
                                                            CIP
                                                            AC

Contents

What Are Constellations?

Look up into the night sky. On a clear night, you can see hundreds of pinpoints of light called stars. Human beings have gazed at these same stars for thousands of years. Some people made shapes and patterns by connecting the brighter stars.

5

Today, we call these patterns constellations.

If you visit a planetarium, you may see a program about constellations. It might show you Orion the Hunter or Gemini the Twins. These constellations may not be as easy to see outdoors as in the planetarium. It does take some practice. Often, people expect to see the exact shape of the hunter or the twins. When they don't, they are disappointed.

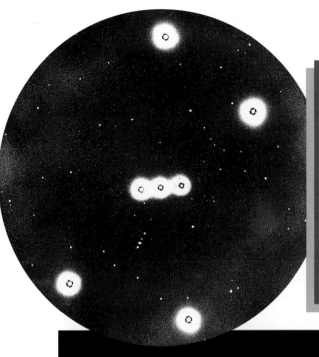

The constellation Orion on the ceiling of a planetarium (left), in the real sky (bottom left), and with the image these stars suggest (bottom right).

RIGEL

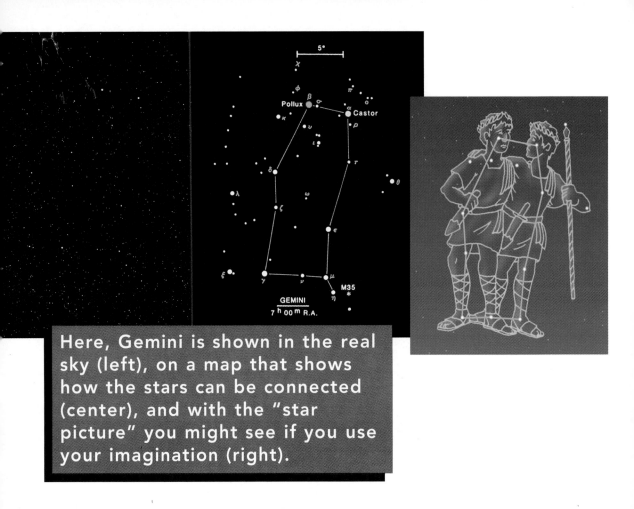

5°

Pollux

Castor

GEMINI
7ʰ 00ᵐ R.A.

M35

Here, Gemini is shown in the real sky (left), on a map that shows how the stars can be connected (center), and with the "star picture" you might see if you use your imagination (right).

Constellations only suggest the things they represent. They were never meant to be exact pictures of people or animals. Ancient people created the constellations to remember important people and events.

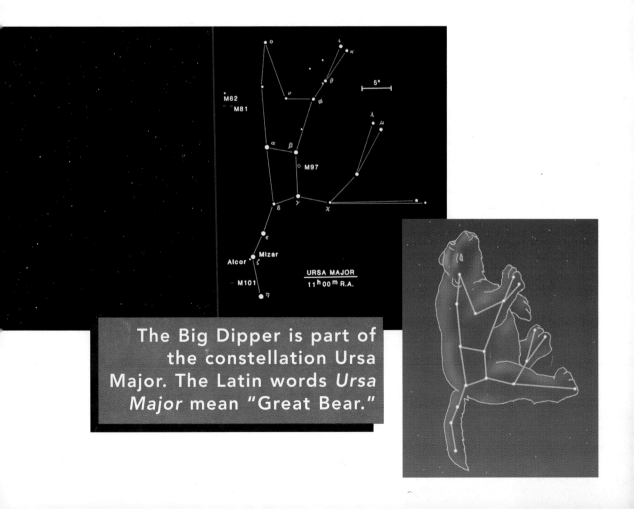

The Big Dipper is part of the constellation Ursa Major. The Latin words *Ursa Major* mean "Great Bear."

The Origin of Constellations

No one knows when people first began to create star pictures in the sky. The earliest record of constellations goes back almost 5,000 years, to ancient Mesopotamia. Later additions were made by Egyptian and Greek astronomers. A total of 48

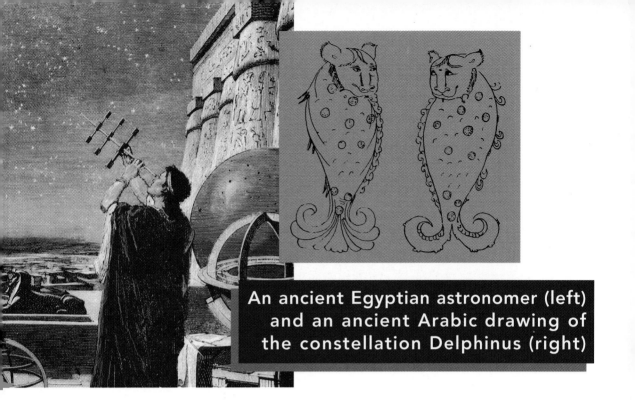

constellations appeared on the first star charts.

In 1928, the International Astronomical Union, an organization made up of astronomers from all over the world, decided on 88 official

11

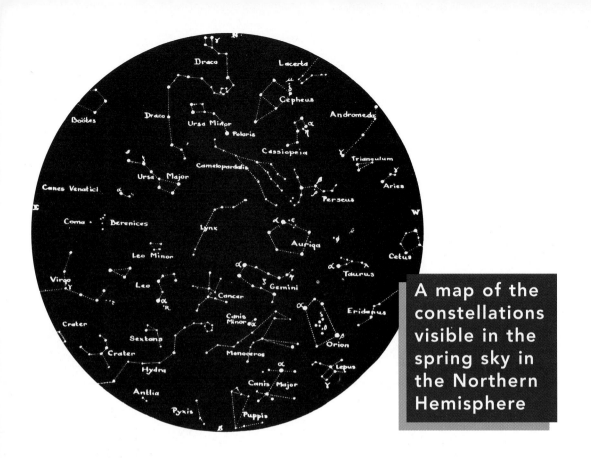

Draco

Lacerta

Cepheus

Draco

Boötes

Andromeda

Ursa Minor

Polaris

Cassiopeia

Triangulum

Camelopardalis

Ursa Major

Aries

Canes Venatici

Perseus

Coma   Berenices

W

Lynx

Auriga

Cetus

Leo Minor

Virgo

Taurus

Leo

Cancer

Gemini

Crater

Eridanus

Canis
Minor

Orion

Sextans

Crater

Monoceros

Lepus

Hydra

Canis Major

Antlia

Pyxis

Puppis

A map of the constellations visible in the spring sky in the Northern Hemisphere

constellations. Many of these were made up of stars visible only in the Southern Hemisphere. Ancient Egyptian and Greek astronomers never knew these stars existed.

Although the stars in a constellation may seem to form a
certain picture, the actual stars
have nothing to do with each

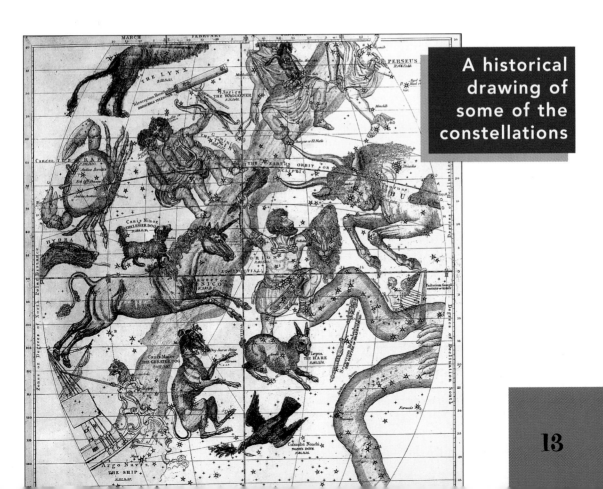

A historical
drawing of
some of the
constellations

13

other, and are all at different distances from us in space. If we could travel out among the stars, different constellations would have to be invented for the new shapes that we could find. Constellations are entirely the creation of human imagination.

In many constellations, the brightest stars have names as well. Star names we use today come from old Arabic ones. For example, Aldebaran, a

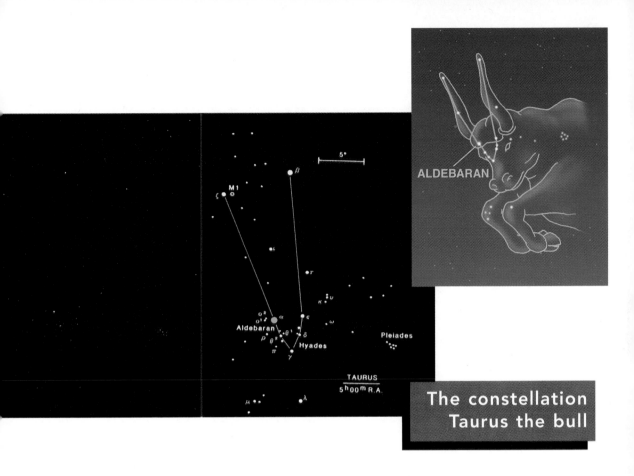

The constellation
Taurus the bull

star in the constellation Taurus,
means the "follower." The star
got its name because it follows
the Pleiades (Seven Sisters)
star cluster across the sky.

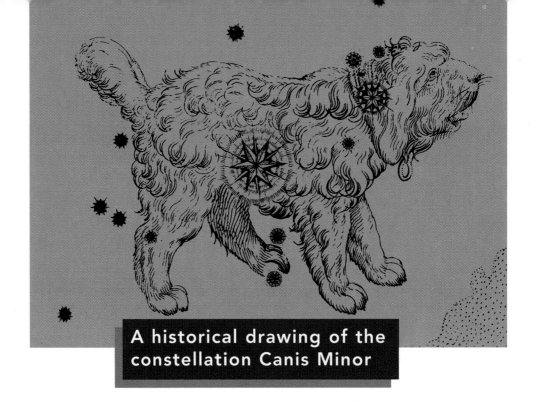

A historical drawing of the constellation Canis Minor

The 88 constellations we now use have Latin names. Ursa Major is the "Great Bear." Canis Minor is the "Little Dog." These names remind us of the cultures and astronomers of long ago.

Uses for Constellations

Ancient people used constellations to help record time. In the course of a year, constellations appeared to move across the sky as the Earth revolved around the Sun. Depending on the season, only certain stars could be seen. People learned to

SPRING

Northern Horizon

Eastern Horizon

Western Horizon

Southern Horizon

The night sky as it appears at 9 p.m. standard time on April 15.

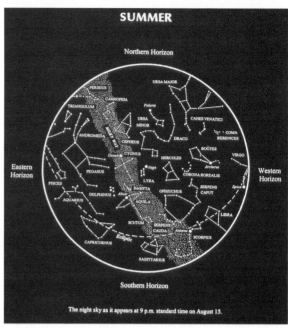

SUMMER

Northern Horizon

Eastern Horizon

Western Horizon

Southern Horizon

The night sky as it appears at 9 p.m. standard time on August 15.

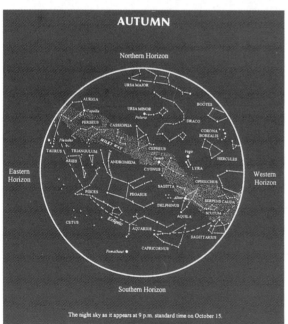

AUTUMN

Northern Horizon

Eastern Horizon

Western Horizon

Southern Horizon

The night sky as it appears at 9 p.m. standard time on October 15.

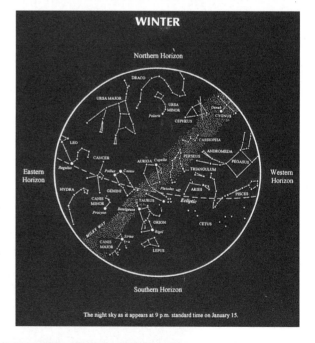

WINTER

Northern Horizon

Eastern Horizon

Western Horizon

Southern Horizon

The night sky as it appears at 9 p.m. standard time on January 15.

The constellations we are able to see change as the seasons change.

depend upon these stars as a sign of the changing seasons.

The brightest star, Sirius, part of the constellation Canis Major, was seen in the winter. A bright star named Antares,

Antares is the brightest star in the constellation Scorpius.

part of Scorpius, could always be seen in the summer. When Regulus in the constellation Leo appeared in the eastern sky, it was the first sign of spring. In the fall, Pegasus was high in the northeastern sky.

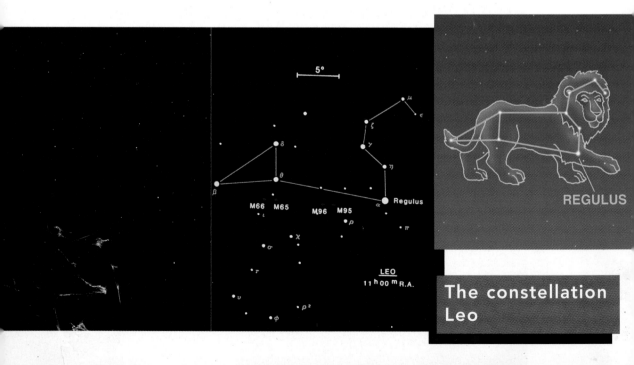

5°

δ
θ
β
M66 M65   M96 M95
•ι   •ρ
•χ
•σ
•τ
•υ
•ρ² •φ

μ
ε
ζ
γ
η

Regulus
α
•π

LEO
11ʰ00ᵐR.A.

REGULUS

The constellation Leo

Skywatchers noticed that from spring to summer, the Sun would rise just a little farther north each day. The same was true from fall to winter, only this time the Sun rose a little farther to the south of east each day.

The stars also appeared to move across the sky from the beginning to the end of each night. As the Earth turned on its axis, some stars rose while others set. People could look at the sky and tell both time and season by reading the patterns in the night.

Though some stars rise and set, others are visible all night long. A star seen all night long is close to the north

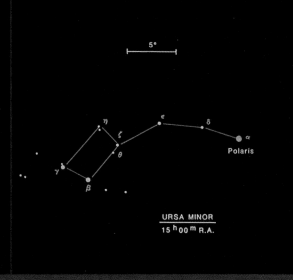

5°

η
ε
δ
ζ
α
θ
Polaris
γ
β

URSA MINOR
15ʰ00ᵐ R.A.

Polaris is the tip of the "handle" of the Little Dipper. The Little Dipper is part of the constellation Ursa Minor ("Little Bear").

pole in the sky. There is one star, Polaris, that is so close to the pole it doesn't seem to move at all! That is why Polaris is sometimes called the North Star—it is always in

For thousands of years, constellations have helped people tell direction.

the north. For centuries, the North Star has helped people tell direction.

Ancient people saw that as the Sun travels across the sky, it moves through only a certain group of constellations.

This imaginary path in the sky was named the zodiac. It is divided into twelve sections, each of which is named after a different constellation.

Along the edge of the circle on this star map is the belt of twelve constellations called the zodiac.

What Did People See in the Sky?

People see the stars differently from different places on Earth. A person in the Southern Hemisphere sees the constellations upside down from their position as seen in the Northern Hemisphere. It is no wonder that different cultures saw different pictures in the stars!

Modern astronomy often uses names taken from Greek mythology for the constellations. The ancient Greeks used the stars to represent their gods and heroes, such as Zeus and Hercules. Parents would show their children the four bright stars of Pegasus and tell of a flying horse. The stars of Taurus reminded them of the legend when Zeus took the form of a bull.

To the Chinese, constellations told stories of everyday people, of great generals in

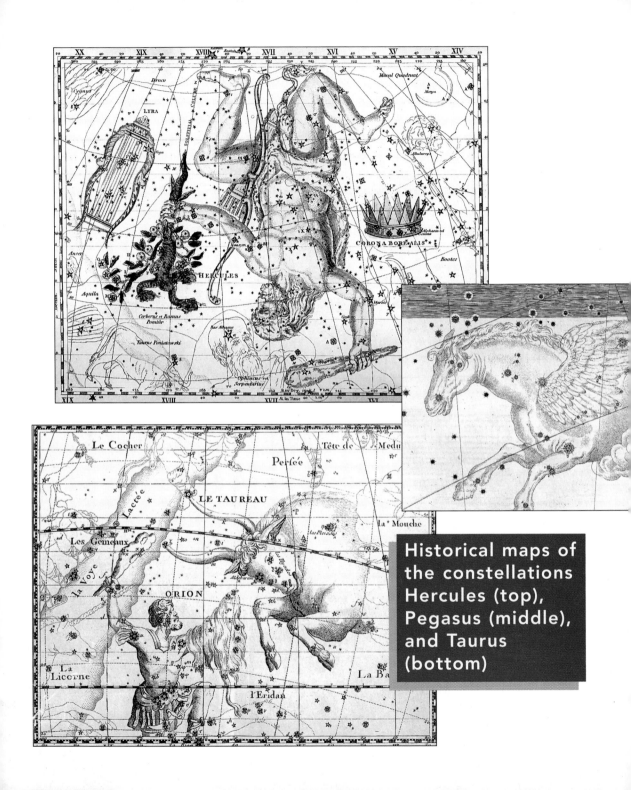

Historical maps of the constellations Hercules (top), Pegasus (middle), and Taurus (bottom)

battle, or of royal parades. These stars and their stories are used as a calendar to predict seasonal changes.

The ancient Egyptians had many myths and gods represented in the stars. The brightest star in the sky, Sirius, represented the goddess Isis.

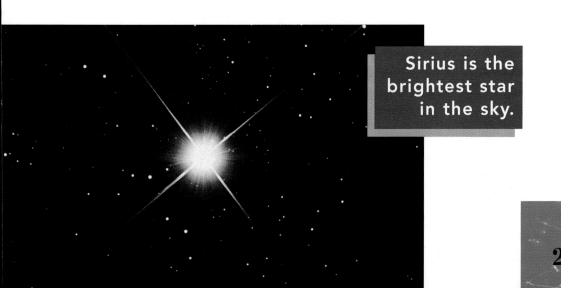

Sirius is the brightest star in the sky.

When Sirius rose in the eastern sky just before sunrise, it was thought that the Nile River would soon flood. This would bring new life to Egypt.

The Pleiades (Seven Sisters) star cluster was important to many African peoples. The Masai of East Africa saw this cluster as a herd of cattle. When it was seen in the sky, the rainy season was near. The Bantu people of Southern Africa saw the Pleiades as a

The constellation we call the Pleiades (above) is important to the Masai people of East Africa (right).

plow. When it rose just after sunset, it was time for plowing and planting crops.

Among Native Americans, the Cherokee tell legends of the Dog Stars. They speak of a journey through the sky made by departed souls. On this journey, they must pass two barking dogs, the stars we call Sirius and Antares. If the departed soul feeds only the first dog and not the second, it will be trapped between the two forever.

Finding Constellations

It's best to start with easy-to-find constellations. If you live north of the equator, start with the Big Dipper. Look in the general direction of north. There you'll see seven fairly bright stars. Four of these form a bowl shape, and three form a bent handle. The

middle star of the handle is
really two stars. If you can see
both, you have perfect vision.

Once you have found the
Big Dipper, you can find
Polaris—the North Star. The
two brightest stars in the Big

Dipper's bowl point to it. A line drawn through both pointer stars will connect straight to Polaris at any time of the night, on any clear night of the year.

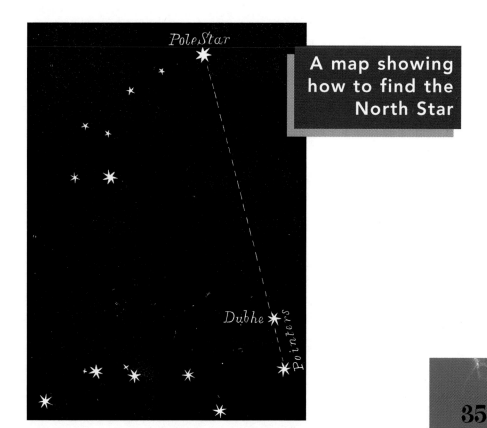

Pole Star

Dubhe

Pointers

A map showing how to find the North Star

The constellation
Cassiopeia

After you have found
Polaris, look for Cassiopeia,
the Queen. Cassiopeia is
always on the opposite side of
the North Star from the Big

Dipper, and its five brightest stars form a "W" shape.

In winter, you can look to the south for Orion the Hunter. In December, at 9:00 P.M., Orion should be directly south. Look halfway up, and you should see three bright stars in a row. These stars mark Orion's belt. Follow the belt up and to the right. This will bring you to Taurus the Bull. Now go back to Orion's belt and look down and to the

Winter

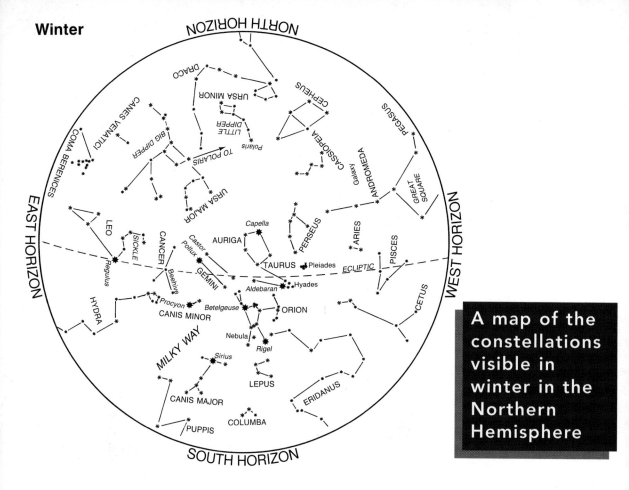

A map of the constellations visible in winter in the Northern Hemisphere

left. Here is Canis Major, the Big Dog, with the star Sirius, the brightest of all nighttime stars. From there you can find many others.

Where Do the Stars Go During the Day?

Have you ever wondered why you can't see stars in the daytime? Stars are in the sky both day and night, but bright sunlight wipes out the light from the stars.

The number of stars we see at night also depends on whether we are viewing the stars from a city or from the country. Near cities, street lights drown out most of the fainter stars. This effect is called light pollution.

If you live south of the equator, the Southern Cross is fun to find. Look for two very bright stars close to each other. These are Alpha Centauri and Beta Centauri. They point to the south toward the Southern Cross. The Southern Cross is very famous. It appears on the flags of both Australia and New Zealand.

In the Southern Hemisphere, the constellations of the zodiac are usually bright, and found

The two bright stars on the right side of this photograph are Alpha Centauri (left) and Beta Centauri (right). The Southern Cross appears on the flag of Australia (inset above).

high overhead. In July, Scorpius, with its fishhook-shaped tail, is easily seen. The Milky Way is very bright and beautiful here.

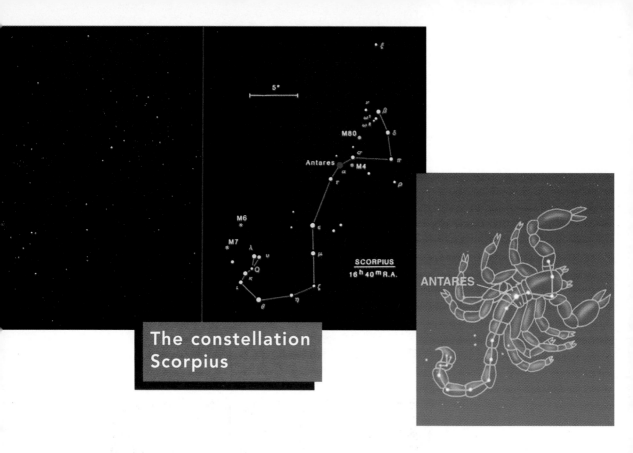

The constellation
Scorpius

Once you learn to spot a few constellations, you have made friends for life. The stars that you see as a young person will still be there when you are old. When you see these stars, you may remember what your parents told you about them. You may tell these same tales to your children. When you do, you will be keeping alive the stories of the stars.

The constellations Orion, Gemini, and Cancer can be found in this photograph.

To Find Out More

Here are some additional resources to help you learn more about constellations:

 **Books**

Branley, Franklyn. **The Big Dipper.** Harper Trophy, 1991.

Chartrand, Mark R. **Skyguide.** Golden Press, 1992.

Gibson, Bob. **The Astronomer's Sourcebook.** Woodbine House, 1992.

Krupp, E.C. **The Big Dipper and You.** Morrow Junior Books, 1989.

Manzel, Donald H., and Jay M. Pasachoff. **A Field Guide to the Stars and Planets.** Houghton Mifflin, 1983.

Pasachoff, Jay M. **Peterson's First Guide to Astronomy.** Houghton Mifflin, 1988.

Rey, H.A. **Find the Constellations.** Houghton Mifflin, 1988.

Rey, H.A. **The Stars: A New Way to See Them.** Houghton Mifflin, 1983.

VanCleave, Janice. **Astronomy for Every Kid: 101 Easy Experiments that Really Work.** John Wiley and Sons, 1991.

Zim, Herbert, Robert H. Baker, and Mark R. Chartrand. **Stars.** Golden Press, 1985.

 **Organizations**

 **Online Sites**

Astronomical Society of the Pacific
1290 24th Avenue
San Francisco, CA 94122
http://www.physics.sfsu.edu/asp

Junior Astronomical Society
58 Vaughan Gardens
Ilford Essex IG1 3PD
England

The Planetary Society
5 North Catalina Avenue
Pasadena, CA 91106
email: *tps.lc@genie.geis.com*

The Planetary Studies Foundation

http://homepage.interaccess.com/~jpatpsf/>.

Constellations and Their Stars

http://www.astro.wisc.edu/~dolan/constellations

45

Important Words

astronomer scientist who studies the stars and planets

equator imaginary line that circles the Earth exactly halfway between the North Pole and South Pole; it divides the Earth into Northern and Southern hemispheres

Latin language of the ancient Romans

Mesopotamia an ancient land that is present-day Iran and Iraq

Milky Way band of soft light seen across the sky at night, made up of stars too far away for the eye to see them separately

mythology collection of traditional stories, usually about a culture's gods or heroes

orbit to circle around

planetarium building in which there is a device for projecting the images of stars and planets on a dome-shaped ceiling

Zeus king of the ancient gods of Greece

Index

Meet the Authors

Paul and Diane Sipiera are husband and wife who share the same interests in science and nature. Paul is a professor of geology and astronomy at William Rainey Harper College in Palatine, Illinois. Diane is the director of education for the Planetary Studies Foundation of Algonquin, Illinois.

When they are not studying or teaching science, Diane and Paul can be found working on their farm in Galena, Illinois, with their daughters Andrea and Paula Frances.